Forex for Beginners

A Guide to Develop Your Forex Trading Skills and Knowledge

© Copyright 2017 Connection Books Club- All Rights Reserved.

This document is presented with the desire to provide reliable, quality information about the topic in question and the facts discussed within. This Book is sold under the assumption that neither the publisher or the author should be asked to provide the services discussed within. If any discussion, professional or legal, is otherwise required a proper professional should be consulted.

The reproduction, duplication or transmission of any of the included information is considered illegal whether done in print or electronically. Creating a recorded copy or a secondary copy of this work is also prohibited unless the action of doing so is first cleared through the Publisher and condoned in writing. All rights reserved.

Any information contained in the following pages is considered accurate and truthful and that any liability through inattention or by any use or misuse of the topics discussed within falls solely on the reader. There are no cases in which the Publisher of this work can be held responsible or be asked to provide reparations for any loss of monetary gain or other damages which may be caused by following the presented information in any way shape or form.

The following information is presented purely for informative purposes and is therefore considered universal. The information presented within is done so without a contract or any other type of assurance as to its quality or validity.

Any trademarks which are used are done so without consent and any use of the same does not imply consent or permission was gained from the owner. Any trademarks or brands found within are purely used for clarification purposes and no owners are in anyway affiliated with this work.

Table of Contents

- Introduction 1
- How Forex Works 5
- How You Start Trading Currency 16
- Understanding The Jargon Of Forex Professionals 21
- Trading Psychology 39
- What To Do In A Bull Or Bear Market 48
- Fundamental Trading Analysis 51
- Technical Trading Analysis 57
- Developing A Forex Strategy That Works For You 63
- Pitfalls To Avoid In Forex Trading 67
- Tools That Help Forex Traders 71
- Wrap Up: Forex Overview 76

Introduction

The forex market is considered a mystery, with a lot of confusing parts thrown in by many stock investors and stock brokers. Even some of the top professionals in their investment field stay away from forex. Yet, numerous books can be found on the subject, and hundreds of articles declare that you can learn to trade in the currency market for big returns – so why waste your money in stocks? It is all about perception, knowledge, and desire.

If you desire to learn all you need to know about the forex market, then there is no reason to be afraid of it. Once you gain the basic knowledge of how it works, you can build on that knowledge to learn strategies.

What you do not want to do is get suckered into the thought that there are magic strategies, or that the strategies in this book will work for every investor. In fact, what you should start to realize is that the various trading strategies people try to sell you are not secret at all, and have actually been modified to fit their risk, time frame, and profit requirements.

Your strategy will need to be developed around your personal profit, risk, and time frame requirements. If you want a long-term investment, with little involvement in the day, then someone's 10-minute trading strategy is not going to work for you. However, if you want a high-risk, high-reward, 10-minute trading strategy, you can use another person's strategy, modify it to your investment amount and make a profit.

To make this happen, you need to know the professional forex jargon, what it means when someone says fundamental versus technical trading analysis, and what the G7 are. For those with this basic knowledge, the harder concepts will come easier.

There is no pressure in this book. You don't have to read through the entire thing in an hour and start trading. In fact, those who read a chapter, assess what they have learned, and then try out a few of the examples found later on in strategies, will have more success.

Read at your own pace. Utilize the tools available to you, and above all else, trade with real money only when you are satisfied with your profit/loss ratio combined with consistency. An inconsistent profit/loss ratio will mean more losses in the end.

You have the controls to say when you are ready to trade. Believe in yourself, in your knowledge, and in your trading strategy. If you can follow these rules—you will succeed.

Thank you for your purchase of this eBook! I hope you enjoy reading this eBook as much as I enjoyed writing it. As part of your purchase, I invite you to join my email subscribers. This FREE subscription lets you receive a newsletter, highlighting the great new books available from Connection Books Club and other exclusive business and self development information. Subscribing is easy, and members receive great deals and fantastic eBooks at a discount! All you need to do is click this link to enter your email:

http://www.connectionbooksclub.com/bonus/

In addition to this great opportunity to subscribe to incredible discounts and our newsletter, as a welcome gift, you'll receive a FREE eBook download! Learn how to secure your financial future with the informative eBook, *Money Management: Learn How to Organize Your Financial Life and Invest in Your Future.* It's yours for FREE once you've enrolled!

http://www.connectionbooksclub.com/bonus/

Welcome to the club, and we hope you enjoy your purchase as well as our FREE welcome gift!

Have you ever wished that you were better with money?

Do you ever find yourself being overwhelmed by the state of your personal finances?

Would you like to become more financially responsible?

Now you can, with **5 Reasons to Invest in Money Management: Learn How to Organize Your Financial**

Life and Invest in Your Future, a short self-help book that is packed with information on how to make the most of your financial situation.

If you want to be able to lower your interest rates, learn up to date money management strategies and turn your financial situation into one of prosperity and stability, then you'll find the answers inside, with solid advice that includes:

- Strategies which are designed for the average person
- Your options for retirement
- Hacks for navigating the grocery store's subtle spending traps
- Ways to pay less than you owe on credit cards and other outstanding debts
- Finding freedom with financial stability

Suitable for complete novices, **5 Reasons to Invest in Money Management** is a book that will transform the way you look at and deal with your finances.

Download a free copy and start investing in your future today! http://www.connectionbooksclub.com/bonus/

Prosperity is waiting for **YOU**!

How Forex Works

The forex market, foreign exchange currency market, FX market, or currency exchange is often a mystery to investors. To help you learn the market, you need to know how it works. The topics that will teach you how it works are:

- Exploring the history of currency
- What decentralized means
- The relevancy of the interbank system
- Who you are in the big picture
- What you trade and when
- Currency movement

Exploring the History of Currency

Currency is how we represent wealth. It is a functional, tangible asset that came into being when the exchange of goods and services needed a better system. The concept of currency has existed for 10,000 years or more, according to historians. In times of old, items of value were traded for other items of need. The bartering system would allow food, weapons, tools, property, materials, adornments, clothing, and household items to be traded for certain items like livestock, metals, grains, and eventually silver and gold.

It was in the 7th millennium BC that coins were fashioned in Western and Central Asia. At this time, gold, tin, and copper were highly important. By the 3rd millennium BC, gold bars created in standardized weights were used as "commodity currencies" to gain items that were desired. The Kingdom of Lydia is thought to be the first country to have coins of silver and gold for the trading of goods. China developed paper currency separately from Lydia and Greece. The Chinese created rounded coins with Chinese characters on them. They also started manufacturing paper notes that would guarantee they had money. At first, the paper was used for credit notes.

The concept took hold in the known world because it was a lighter means of bringing "currency" to an exchange of goods. By 1150, Europe established the first paper mill to start creating currency. It was not until the 1500s that a banking system was put in place to regulate "money." Banks formed as a means of providing receipts for people making currency deposits. Banknotes, such as bonds, started to emerge in the next century, along with the Bank of England. At this time, money was backed by the amount of gold in reserve.

The notes could be exchanged for gold at a certain amount. There were problems with the currency system, which are still around today. Counterfeiting increased with the increase of paper currency. It was also determined in the 1940s that the gold standard could no longer support the currency system. Currency value couldn't keep up with the amount of gold in existence and two world wars affected the current system in place.

In 1944, 45 countries came together and developed the Bretton Woods Accord. It stated that the strong US dollar would be used to back world currencies, instead of only gold.

Gold would still back currency, but in this case the dollar was considered more valuable given the country's reserves and ability to keep gold in reserves. There was not enough money to keep pace with the demand, so in 1973, the US could no longer keep the "gold standard" for their money.

Today, the forex market is not backed by gold or any one particular asset. Instead, the government's creditworthiness and public sentiment determines the value of currency, as do supply and demand.

Electronic trading has also changed how much the currency market will fluctuate in terms of the currency value. Investors are able to look at multiple currencies, political, economic, and major events, as well as past data to assess if one currency is going to weaken against another.

What Decentralized Means

The forex market is considered a decentralized trading market. There is no regulatory body that oversees the entire world's currency system. Each country, with its own currency, has the central or federal banks to regulate the financial market. Brokers offering investment opportunities do not have to be registered in each country in order to help you trade currencies. They just have to follow proper financial regulations in their own country. This setup means there is no centralized location providing forex trades. The stock market is centrally traded based on places like the London Stock Exchange and Wall Street's New York Stock Exchange. Technology allows you and other investors to buy and sell currencies through different dealers, who deal with different banks, who sell currency based on the interbank system.

The Relevance of the Interbank System

The Interbank Market is an online financial system set up for currency trading between banks and financial institutions. It does not contain the retail investor or small trading parties. The interbank system is done through banks, for large customers of the bank, such as the bank's own accounts. A government can use a bank to place an exchange of one currency to another in order to pay a debt.

The Interbank Market tends to conduct 50% of the forex trades that occur in a year. The floating rate system, where supply and demand determine the value of a currency helps allow bankers to speak and agree on an exchange rate for the transaction.

To make a trade within the interbank system, a bank such as Citicorp, JP Morgan Chase, Deutsche Bank, or HSBC needs to place a minimum size of at least $5 million. Single deals can often average $1 billion. Interbank counterparties make two way prices at which they are willing to buy or sell a given currency, and are referred to as market makers. Institutional market participants such as hedge funds may trade in equally large amounts, but they are only on one side of the market at any given time. They are thus referred to as market takers, as they only take prices.

Electronic dealing systems such as EBS, Reuters, and Bloomberg facilitate interbank transactions by allowing institutions to communicate with each other instantaneously. A bank such as JPMorgan Chase will post the rate at which it is willing to buy or sell a currency, and a second bank such as Wells Fargo can deal on its rate. These transactions happen in the blink of an eye. Smaller banks that have trading relationships with the larger banks can also buy and sell with them at the posted rates via the dealing system. Retail customers - both companies and individuals - buy and sell with the banks rather than on the interbank system.

Typically, in a retail bank deal, you are ordering a certain amount of currency for travel or to make a payment to an overseas vendor. Transactions are for smaller amounts and generally incur larger fees on a percentage basis.

ECN stands for electronic communications network. It is an online banking option and is increasingly dominant in foreign exchange, versus a broker who may execute phone transactions. Both traditional phone brokers and electronic trading services put buyers and sellers together in exchange for a transaction fee.

Market makers decrease their risk by using a spread, which is called the bid-ask spread. You may see between 0.0002 and 0.0005 difference between the bid and ask price for a currency such as the euro or the British pound vs. the U.S. dollar. For Japanese yen, the spread will likely be 0.01 to 0.03 because of the way that the currency is quoted. The 0.0005 difference in price is the fee the market maker will earn for the transaction.

Who You Are in the Big Picture

In a financial market, where you have all types of investors, it is important to realize the big picture determines how currencies are traded. You are going to embark on a journey where $5.3 trillion of trade volume is seen per day! The NYSE (New York Stock Exchange) only deals in $22.4 billion per day. Yes, the NYSE volume is nothing to sneeze at, if you will only see $1 million in your lifetime. But, in the financial arena, it is small potatoes.

Based on the fact that governments, central banks, big banks, small banks, corporations, and investors are all in the mix, trading currency, it can seem pretty unlikely that you fit into the big picture at all. But you do. Your trades can carry weight, depending on who else is buying or selling the same currency. You can be a market player with big lots that changes a trend. It all depends on whether you wish to invest with leverage to gain larger lot sizes, or if you make a tiny movement into an exploding movement.

What you Trade and When

The main pieces are what you do when you make a trade. We have examined the larger movements between banks, brokers, market makers, and you in a broad sense. A part of how the forex market works is based on what you are doing when you buy or sell currency on a broker's website.

You are usually going to see bid/ask on a currency page. Bid means buy and ask means sell. If you wish to buy a currency, then you select bid to purchase a currency at the market price. If you wish to sell a currency, then you select ask to sell a currency at the market price.

However, you are probably wondering what all this means. What are you really trading when you select bid or ask? Is it just one currency, multiple currencies, and what about the difference between the bid and ask?

The forex market works with currency pairs: GBP/USD, EUR/USD, USD/JPY, USD/CAD, USD/CHF, NZD/USD, and AUD/USD. These are the top-traded currency pairs in the market. Each currency pair has a base currency and a quote currency.

The base currency is the first currency in the pairing, so for GBP/USD, the base currency is the GBP. The USD/JPY pairing has the USD as the base currency. The quote currency is the second currency represented by the abbreviations. This means the USD is the quote currency for the GBP/USD, but the JPY is the quote currency for the USD/JPY currency pair.

The terms "bid" and "offer" generally refer to the base currency. For example, to "hit the bid" in EUR/USD means to deal on the left side of the quote and sell EUR/buy USD. If you "take the offer" or "pay the offer," you buy EUR and sell USD. In USD/JPY, by contrast, you would buy USD on the right hand side (the offer) and sell it on the left (the bid).

A golden rule of forex is what the base currency represents. The base currency always represents 1.000. For the GBP, it means 1 GBP. The quote currency can change. For example, when looking up the GBP/USD for the current day during the writing of this, the GBP/USD price was 1.3136. If you walked into a bank with 1 GBP and exchanged it for USD, you would receive 1.3136 USD. If you walked into the bank to exchange 1 USD for Japanese yen, you would receive 101.80 JPY. Tomorrow, if you go to the same bank, you might find you can trade 1 USD for 102.50 JPY. The quote currency is the rate that changes, even in milliseconds, as investors buy and sell a currency pair.

The market is based on the supply of a currency and the demand for that currency. Are investors buying USD and selling GBP or selling USD and buying GBP?

To be slightly convoluted, if you bid on a currency pair, then you buy the base currency and sell the quote currency. If you select ask, you sell the base currency and buy the quote currency.

This is the area that often confuses the new investor. They are unsure what they are truly buying or selling. If necessary, write it out and post it near your computer, so you can keep up with it.

The forex market works differently than the stock market in many ways, including the times when you can trade. You might have heard the forex market referred to as the 24/7 market.

It is a financial market that is nearly open 24 hours a day, 7 days a week. You're probably asking how that can be. It's simple. The forex market is open based on when the other countries' financial markets open. When New Zealand wakes up, they open the first financial market. The timing of New Zealand waking up is nearly the same time as the United States financial markets closing. So in essence, when one country goes to sleep another is waking up. As time arrives for new countries to wake, you also have some countries that are in their mid-day or afternoon. For example, the morning in the USA coincides with the open afternoon hours in the UK. This overlap in markets can create some of the busiest times to trade.

**Remember that time overlaps produce the most volume in the forex market because this is when you are going to want to trade. You want to take advantage of when other investors are in the market because this allows more liquidity, volume, and volatility to move the currency values. In downtimes, when other countries are going to sleep and new ones are waking, you might see a pip or two movements. In high volume times, you can earn 100 pips or more on one trade. One more thing to note is that the financial markets might be open, but your broker might be closed for trading, because of holidays, technical, and weather-related issues. So, before trading make sure that at least some of these issues do not interrupt your trading.

If you do place a trade and the fact that these types of events cannot be foreseen or predicted contribute to the importance of leaving orders, especially stop-loss orders to protect you when you may not be able to execute a transaction yourself.

Currency Movement

Forex works based on how the currency value changes based on the two currencies in a pair. It is generally thought that if one currency in the pair is increasing in value, then the other currency is decreasing. It doesn't have to work like that, and in fact, this is another point of confusion for new investors.

When the quote currency increases in price, the quote currency is weakening against the base currency. Remember, if you have 1 of the base currency and the quote currency is 1.3136, you are obtaining 1.3136 for every 1 of the base currency. You are getting more of the quote currency for each 1 of the base currency. In reverse if you are selling the quote currency, then in reality you have to sell more of the quote currency to get 1 of the base currency.

Rather than dwell on this confusing point, simply know three things:

- The base currency can be strengthened against the quote currency
- The quote currency can be strengthened against the base currency
- The base and quote currency can be moving in the same direction as each other in terms of strengthening or weakening

When the base currency is getting stronger, the quote currency may be weakening, thus there will be an uptrend in the chart.

When the quote currency is getting stronger, the quote currency will be in a downward trend. As an explanation, let's say that the quote currency starts the day at 1.3106 and ends the day at 1.3001; this is a downward trend, which indicates that it will take less of a quote currency to buy a base currency.

Depending on whether the quote currency is gaining or losing strength, it can be in a downtrend or uptrend, along with the base currency. In this situation, where the two currencies are moving in the same direction, it is a matter of which currency is moving quicker. If the base currency is still stronger overall than the quote currency, the trend will be up, versus a stronger overall quote currency. If the currency pair is moving nearly the same speed in terms of strength or weakness, you may see a sideways trading pattern. The charted prices will not be moving much.

In forex, a pip is the smallest amount that the price of a currency can change. If a quote currency changes from 1.3136 to 1.3137, there has been a change of 0.0001 or one pip change. If a currency is only quoted to two decimal places, such as the yen vs. the dollar, and the price changes from 108.67 to 108.68, that also is one pip.

To Sum It Up

The forex market works based on the free market trade setup and decentralized concept of the system. Central banks and large banks help determine the day's currency value based on how the market closed the day before and the anticipated openings of the world FX market. These prices are then sold to large and small banks, who sell to you. You buy or sell based on the anticipated value increase or decrease of one currency against another currency. When you start trading, you need to determine if the quote currency is going to weaken or strengthen against the base currency to make money. Money is made from the pip increase or decrease you see in the currency price.

How You Start Trading Currency

Understanding the value of a pip is imperative for your trading success; however, before you delve further into specific forex jargon, you'll want to have a trading account. A trading account can open doors to trading tools that will help you learn how to trade successfully.

- Explore the various brokers
- Determine which currencies you wish to trade
- Sign up for an account
- Fund the account

Explore the Various Brokers

With a decentralized market, there are numerous brokers and market makers to research. The forex market is regulated to a degree, but it is also easy for someone to start buying and selling forex positions without proper regulations. You want to avoid being scammed, as this happens in countries with fewer regulations in trading.

To choose a broker, you need to know which well-known companies in the trading circle offer forex. Find out which ones you can trust to provide you properly regulated services. To find out which ones you can trust, visit your government websites, search for financial trading information, and you will see who has been listed as a registered forex trader. The CFTC or Commodity Futures

Trading Commission is one website to visit for this information. http://www.cftc.gov/Contact/index.htm

This site is provided to research backgrounds of brokers. http://smartcheck.cftc.gov/

This is a link to a list of brokers that are not being overseen by CFTC and could be a risk to investors.

http://smartcheck.gov/redlist/

Besides checking to see if the broker is properly regulated and has no complaints against it, you will want to research other factors.

- The lot sizes you can trade.
- How easy their platform is to use.
- The tools they offer.

Lot sizes can be as small as 1,000 units. This is a micro unit. A mini lot is 10,000 and a standard lot size is 100,000 units. There are macro units of 1 million units. Some companies offer Nano units, which are 100 units of a currency.

The lot size you want is going to be based on your trading ability. For individuals with a small starting capital you will need smaller units to ensure you are not spending all your capital in one trade.

Some electronic platforms are more difficult to use than others. It is not fun or even appropriate to find yourself in a troubling situation because you are unable to use the platform. If you are sitting down to trade, but you are having trouble sending in an order, you could lose money. Worse, you could enter a position that is suddenly opposite the current trend because it took too long for you to get the order filled. It is far better to find a platform you can learn or already use. The good news is a lot of forex brokers offer a trial period with a paper money account. You are able to poke around their software, determine if you like it, and then fund a real money account when you are ready.

Tools in forex will be discussed in detail later. What you need to know is that you should have access to the basic tools: paper money account, charts, automated signals, news updates, and charting software.

Determine which Currencies you want to Trade

Every country has a currency they use. Europe has the euro, which is used by most of the western European countries and some eastern European countries. However, not all currencies of each country are worth trading. Some currencies are so weak that there is no volume or too much volatility in the currency movement. These currencies can be dangerous to trade, create losses, or simply be too boring to make any money from. If you are going to look beyond the G7 currency pairs, you may need to find a specialty broker. Many of the brokers are unwilling to offer more than the top currency pairs that generate the most volume and liquidity for traders. Other brokers recognize that there are some G20 currency pairs worth trading.

Sign up for an Account

After you have exhausted all research avenues into the brokers available in your country, who have proper regulation and no major complaints against them, it is time to set up your account.

You will be asked to enter a name, address, identification number, and other identifying information. Many brokers will take a scan of your driver's license, social security or ID number card, and a voided check to verify your identity and bank account. Sometimes, if the image is not clear enough, you may need to mail in additional identification verification.

This process varies slightly for different brokers. It is only when your ID has been verified that you will be able to verify your bank account information to set up electronic transfers between your broker account and your bank account. In the meantime, you can be learning the paper money side of your account, as well as how the platform works.

Funding your Account

As stated, to fund your account, you need to verify your identity and bank information. Once this is done, you can make a transfer via online portals to get your account ready to trade. Even if you have money in your account, you have a ways to go before you should be trading with real money. You want to practice strategies and learn as much as you can before you actually start to trade.

It is also important to determine how much you are going to fund your account with. There are some general rules to follow:

- Never use money you cannot spare to invest. If you need the $10,000 you are going to fund your account with as an emergency fund in the event of job loss, you shouldn't risk it in the market.

- You should not take out an equity loan just to invest in forex.
- Only use money you are willing to lose.

If you do not have money you are willing to lose, then you should not fund your account with it. When there is too much to lose, you can start to make mistakes.

To Sum It Up

Research is required before you start trading in the forex market. Not only should you know what you are doing when it comes to risking your money, but you also need to know you can trust your broker. There are government sites that show you broker firms, if they are registered, and if there are any complaints against the broker. It is imperative that you look over these sites and choose from an acceptable broker list. You will then be able to set up an account and get it funded.

Enjoying your eBook so far? Take a moment to subscribe to our FREE newsletter for incredible discounts, books giveaways, and VIP offers!

> http://www.connectionbooksclub.com/bonus/

All we need is your email, and you'll be set up to receive more of the eBooks you can't wait to read.

Understanding The Jargon Of Forex Professionals

The key terms in this chapter are those you will often see in forex books and articles. These are the words you want to know, as you begin to learn new strategies, because they will be used to describe how the strategy works, what it works on, as well as how the market works overall.

- Volatility
- Volume
- Liquidity
- Pips
- Pip Spread
- Margin Call
- G7
- G20
- Bull Market
- Bear Market
- Risk-Reward Ratio
- Profit/Loss
- Trading Plan
- Restricted Currencies
- Spot Forex Contracts

Volatility

Volatility is a professional investment term you are going to see often in forex discussions. Volatility is considered the "degree of variation" between trading prices over a certain period of time, and is measured based on the standard "deviation of returns." Basically, it is a statistical measurement that helps you understand the variance between the returns for currency pairs. More importantly, volatility will show if there is an uncertainty or risk with regards to the currency pair's value. A high volatility translates as a value which is spread out over a larger value range, so the price will change drastically in a short time frame versus a low volatility where the value is not going to fluctuate quickly, but over a longer period of time.

Volume

Volume is the amount of "shares" or units that are traded in the market. When there is a buyer, there is always a seller, thus transactions determine the total volume. If you have only five transactions in a day, the volume is low. For the G7 currencies, hundreds of thousands of trades can be placed in a day, which means a high volume. High volume can strengthen or weaken a currency pair's value based on the majority movement of the trades being placed. During one move, the more volume or interest in the current trend, the more significant the move is going to be.

Liquidity

In forex, you are dealing with money. Cash is considered the most liquid asset to exist, which also makes the forex market the most liquid of trading markets. When talking about trading, you want to understand market liquidity. Market liquidity is a value placed on how much money is in the market at the time. A higher market liquidity means there is a higher trade volume or a higher interest in that specific asset.

Pips

A pip is 0.0001 for currencies that are quoted to 4 decimal places, such as the euro, British pound, or Swiss franc. The Japanese yen is quoted to 2 decimal places, so one pip is .01. If you are assessing a currency pair for profit, you want to determine how much you can make off a pip change. For example, how much is one pip worth? There is a calculation you need to keep in mind as you think about the pairs you are going to trade:

For the pip value, let's assume you are using a standard lot, which is 100,000 units. We'll say we are trading the USD/JPY, where the exchange rate is 119.00. You would use the calculation ER (pip/ER) x lot size to gain the value of one pip. If you plug in 119.80 (0.01/119.80) x100, 000 you would get that 1 pip is worth $8.34

For other currencies, the calculation is ER (0.0001/ER) x100, 000 equals pip value. Let's say you are looking for the GBP/USD price per pip: 1.3136 (0.0001/1.3136) x 100, 000 equals $10 per pip. When the USD is the quote currency, the pip value can be $1 up to $100 depending on the lot size. For a standard lot size, you will always see $10 as the pip value, where the dollar is the quote currency.

Spread

The spread is where the broker is going to make money. It is the difference between the bid and ask price. If you see 1.3136 as the bid price, then you may see 1.3141 as the ask price. The sell price is usually between 2 and 5 pips more than the buy price because you expect the ask price to go down. Spreads can widen sharply in times of high market volatility.

Margin and Margin Call

You can use margin to increase what you have to invest.

Margin is the use of leverage to increase the account to the lot size that you are able to trade. It is a loan secured loan from a broker on which you must pay interest. A request for a margin account must be approved and is dependent on credit ratings and available security.

For example, let's say you have $1,000 in your account, but you need $100,000 to place a trade. You can use margin to "leverage" your account,and borrow the funds you need to trade in the desired lot size. It sounds confusing. As long as you remember that you leverage your account to borrow enough to buy an acceptable lot size, then you will understand part of the concept.

Margin call is when the broker requires you settle your account. If you have placed a trade, where your account has decreased in value to a certain risk point, the broker will ask you to sell your trade or deposit money to cover your current trade. Let's say you used $100,000 to buy 100,000 units of a currency, but you actually invested $50,000 of your own money. You might have a requirement to maintain 25% of that margin amount in your forex account, so if you do not have at least $25,000 as a liquidity balance in the account, you would be asked to close part of the trade or to deposit enough to keep your account at the 25% mark.

In forex, traders often use leverage as a means of trading for a higher profit. The downside is the increased risk that comes from essentially borrowing money to invest. You can have a significant loss that you may not be able to cover without selling your home, car, and all other assets you own.

G7

The group of 7 is comprised of Canada, United States, France, Germany, Italy, Japan, and the United Kingdom. They are also the countries with the major economic advancements, as reported by the International Monetary Fund. To be considered as part of the G7, the countries have more than 64% of the net global wealth, a net national wealth, and high human development index. The countries also represent 46 percent of the global gross domestic products (GDP). It means the G7 have the majority of goods and services produced, when combined.

The stability of the currencies of these countries created G7 pairings that are strong, with high volume, liquidity, and volatility. When the euro was adopted in Europe, France, Italy, and Germany became represented by one currency, opening the door to other currency pairs, with strong economic data and strong GDP results.

Today, the CHF, NZD, and AUD are considered top currencies to trade that will make up the G7 currency pairs. The CHF is the Swiss Franc. The Swiss did not join in using the euro as its natural currency and the CHF is considered a safe haven.

A safe haven currency is one that is bought when the market is in turmoil. It is due to how well the currency is backed by the government. There is faith that the United States Treasury Bills are safe in a troubling economy because the US government backs them, thus the USD is also a safe haven currency. The CHF is backed by a good stock of gold reserves, as well as a trusted government.

G20

Since 1999, there has been a concept of the Group of Twenty. It is an international forum for central bank governors and governments of the major 20 economies. Not all of the G20 are part of the European Union. The countries in this group are Argentina, Brazil, China, India, Indonesia, South Korea, Mexico, Russia, South Africa, Saudi Arabia, Turkey, the UK, USA, Germany, Australia, Canada, France, Italy, Japan, and European Union. These economies make up 85% of the GDP and 80% of the world trade, as well as two-thirds of the earth's population. Many of the currencies represented by these countries can be traded with stable volume, volatility, and liquidity at strong world economic times; however, some currencies are weaker and less interesting to trade than others. Many of the governments have restrictions on the ability to trade. Above all other currencies available in the market to trade, the G20 are the ones you want to compare and understand as possible trading avenues.

Restricted Currencies

Many governments limit trading, and particularly speculation, in their currencies. There are a number of reasons for this: (1) limited availability of dollars in the country and the need to control their allocation; (2) concern about speculators, who could push the forex rate to either stronger or weaker levels than what is considered desirable; (3) a perceived need to limit or control foreign investment in the country; and (4) fear of an exodus of hard currency out of the country when the local currency is under pressure. While currency controls are only enforceable within any given country's borders, restrictive trading rules inhibit the development of a robust forex market.

Many of the world's developing economies have currencies that can only be bought and sold for approved import and export transactions, and often only at rates that are set by the central bank. Currency that has been purchased for an unapproved transaction might be blocked, meaning that the holder can't legally sell it. It's important to keep track of currency regulations, as they can change quickly and without warning.

China is a good example of a country with a very large economy but a limited forex market. The country's $11.4 trillion economy is second in size only to the United States, and its GDP growth of 5.6% in 2016 is far higher, although far below the 7.5% recorded in 2010. However, the People's Bank of China (PBC), the country's central bank, continues to separate the currency into the domestic yuan (CNY) and the offshore yuan (CNH). The domestic yuan can only be bought and sold by local participants, and can only move 2% above or below the official rate. The PBC intervenes regularly to limit the currency's appreciation or depreciation.

The offshore yuan is open to offshore banks and institutions, but the market is thin and relatively few brokers participate. The PBC is known to intervene regularly when the currency moves further or faster than it considers appropriate. The central bank has indicated that it wants to merge the two markets but it is unclear when that might happen. In the meantime, offshore yuan cannot be used within the country.

India is another example of a large and rapidly modernizing economy that does not have a freely traded currency. It's the tenth large economy in the world, with GDP of nearly $2 trillion and an annual growth rate that approaches 5%. However, the Reserve Bank of Indian (RBI), the country's central bank, sharply limits the movement of money into and out of the country. The RBI intervenes regularly to limit the currency's movements, which makes it difficult to trade.

Russia is one of the world's most important countries, both economically and politically, with domestic GDP of more than $2 trillion and some of the world's largest oil and gas reserves. It is also one of the most challenging countries in which to do business, as the rules can change quickly and without notice.

The ruble is usually available to trade through most larger brokerage firms and on electronic foreign exchange platforms. However, the market shuts down periodically when the central bank hikes rates to defend the currency or changes the trading rules. This can leave speculators unable to close positions until the market re-opens, often at a sharply different rate than where it closed.

A final example of an important country with a currency that is not widely traded is Brazil. It boasts the world's seventh largest economy, but a recession that has lasted for several years amid declining worldwide prices for its commodity exports will cut that by an estimated 3.5% in 2016 while inflation hits 9%.

This might seem like an excellent opportunity for a forex trader to short Brazil's currency, the real. But there is a very limited spot market, with domestic transactions limited to government-approved imports, exports, and investments. There is an offshore market for speculative transactions, but here too speculators are put off by rules and exchange rates that can change suddenly and without notice.

Forex traders need to investigate the regulatory environment when choosing to trade an emerging market currency, and keep careful track of any changes. Such currencies can offer excellent profit opportunities, but closed markets and unexpected devaluations can pull the rug out from under unwary investors.

Spot Forex Contracts

A spot contract settles in two business days, with the exception of USD/CAD, which settles the next business day. The settlement date must be a valid business day in the home country of both currencies. This convention means that weekends and holidays can push the number of calendar days until settlement to 5, 6 or even 7 days especially during periods such as Christmas and Easter. Valid euro settlement days are established annually by the European Central Bank (ECB), and do not depend on each country's holiday calendar.

By market convention, money changes hands on the settlement date, not the trade date. This is why even spot forex contracts have credit risk associated with them.

The most actively traded spot pair of currencies is EUR/USD, with approximately 24% of the global total. USD/JPY commands 14% while GBP/USD gets 9%. USD/CHF and USD/CAD round out the top five.

Forward Forex Contracts

A forward contract is any forex deal with a maturity longer than spot. For USD/CAD, that means any deal with a maturity date more than one business day in the future; for all other currency pairs, a forward is more than 3 business days in the future. Like spot transactions, they are done between an investor and a bank or between two banks. Forward contracts are actively traded via brokers and on electronic trading platforms.

Forwards, like spot deals, can settle on any day that is not a holiday or weekend in either home country. As with spot deals, euro holidays are established by the ECB each year, and banks in euro zone countries must abide by that list.

Forward rates are based on the interest rate differential between the two currencies. The spot rate is increased or decreased based on where the yield is higher. When a market participant buys a currency with a higher interest rate for delivery in the future, that means that until the settlement date, that investor is holding the currency with a lower interest rate. The forward rate in this case is thus lower (cheaper) that the spot rate, to compensate the investor.

Forward points are quoted in pips, and the last whole number in the price quote lines up with the far right-hand side of the spot rate. As an example, with EUR/USD spot quoted at 1.3135 on the offer side, the 1 month forward points to buy EUR are quoted as +15.86 (also on the offer side). When calculating the all-in forward rate, the 5 in the points (the last whole number) lines up under the 5 in the spot rate, making the forward points +.001586 and the all-in forward rate is 1.315186 (1.3135 + .001586).

If the investor is selling EUR vs. USD, the spot rate (on the bid side) is 1.3132, and the points are +15.76. The calculation is 1.3132 + .001576 = 1.314776. This is a better rate for a seller than the current spot rate, because he is holding the lower yielding currency until the delivery date.

A forward contract can be for any currency amount. An investor can either take delivery on the contract at maturity, or close it out in advance and take the gain or loss on the transaction.

Futures Contract

Like forwards, the price of futures contracts reflects the spot rate plus or minus forward points, which are derived from the interest rate differential. Unlike forwards, they are traded on commodity markets, which buy and sell the contracts to investors.

Futures contracts are for standardized lots, which vary from market to market, and only settle on certain days of the month. They also are not deliverable, and must be cash settled at or before maturity.

Cross-Currencies

A cross currency transaction is a forex deal in which neither of the two currencies is the U.S. dollar. The three most common crosses include the euro: EUR/GBP, EUR/JPY, and EUR/CHF. Other popular cross trades are GBP/CHF, GBP/JPY, and CHF/JPY, but any two convertible currencies can be traded against each other.

The most popular crosses trade actively on the electronic markets and through brokers. Spreads are somewhat wider than the most active dollar-based pairs (EUR/USD, USD/JPY, GBP/USD), but not usually more than 10-15 pips.

Transactions for pairs that are not actively traded against each other can be tailor-made by brokers or banks, but those spreads are usually far wider. This means that investors need to be very confident of a trade before taking a position, as there's further to go before potential profit can cover the bid-offer spread.

Options

Options are an important component of foreign exchange, but should only be used after an investor is completely comfortable with spot and forward contracts. When used wisely, options can allow an investor to make a large profit with relatively little risk. But they can be extremely dangerous if misused, and brokers often require investors to demonstrate that they understand options before using them.

The two basic options contracts are calls and puts. A call gives its owner the right but not the obligation to buy a currency at a given price (the strike) before the expiration date. A put gives its owner the right but not the obligation to sell a currency at the strike price before the expiration date. Puts and calls are referred to as "plain vanilla" options, as they are the simplest form of the structure.

An investor must pay a premium in order to buy an option. The cost of the option is governed by several factors, which are described below.

1. How far in the future is the expiration date? As a general rule, the further out the expiration date, the higher the price of the option. This is because there is more time during which the market could reach the strike.

2. How close is the strike price to the current forward rate for the expiration date? If the strike is the same as the forward rate, the option is said to be "at the money." If the strike is worse than the forward, the option is "out of the money."

3. What is the volatility of the option? This is a complex statistical measure that reflects how much the value of the underlying asset (in this case, a currency) will change until expiration. Higher volatility results in a higher price for the option, because a greater change in value increases the likelihood that the option will reach or approach its strike price.

Buying an out of the money put or call can be a relatively inexpensive way for an investor to open a new position or hedge an existing one. Let's say that the EUR/USD spot rate is 1.3135 and the 1 month forward rate to buy euros is 1.315186. An investor who wants to go long for that time period can enter into a forward contract. Or, if he thinks that the euro is going higher during that period, he could buy a EUR/USD call that's 5% out of the money (1.3810) for perhaps 2% of the nominal amount of the option, or $2,000 on a $100,000 contract.

Unlike a forward, where the currencies don't change hands until the maturity date, the premium must be paid right away and is a sunk cost of the transaction. If the option expires in the money, the investor can exercise it and take delivery of the currency, or immediately sell the currency back at the then-current spot rate.

But the best part of buying an option is that an investor can make money even if the market doesn't reach the strike. If the market moves close to the strike price, and if the volatility spikes higher, the option will increase in value and the investor can sell it for a profit, without it being in the money.

An investor who is bullish on EUR/USD over a 1 month horizon can buy the EUR/USD forward but protect himself by buying an out of the money put. This protects him against the downside, and the strike (plus the premium cost) becomes the worst case scenario. This tactic allows an investor to eliminate stop-loss orders and be more aggressive in a volatile market.

Options can become dangerous, however, when they are sold instead of bought as they create an obligation rather than a right. In other words, buying a call is the right to buy EUR/USD at the strike, but selling the call is the obligation to sell it at the strike. An investor who sells an option (also known as writing an option) without owning the underlying asset earns the premium but has unlimited downside risk if the option moves in the money.

The sale of options is a strategy that is usually done as part of a more complex structure that either reduces cost or changes the investor's risk profile. They are a topic for the more advanced forex investor.

Bull Market

A bull market is typically considered an optimistic market. It is represented by the bull with horns because the bull thrusts its horns upwards when it attacks. It is generally thought that a bull market shows an increase in volume, liquidity, and volatility in trading because more investors feel confident to trade. The bull market has three phases: expansion, peak, and contraction where economic expansion is usually the reason for a bull market. It means public sentiment is positive that the financial market is steady due to stable economic conditions, so value in financial products increases.

Bear Market

A bear market is when there is a downtrend. Instead of optimism, market investors feel pessimistic. Economic conditions are usually decreasing in strength or stability, so there is worry from the majority of investors that financial products will have value worth trading. In a bear market, investors tend to short sell – meaning they sell their shares and wait to buy them back at a lower price. You can short sell shares you don't own by placing a "sell" trade. There are also possibilities of using options, where you do not have to sell a stock at a specific price, until a certain date or price occurs. Options are complicated, so rather than talking about those in a beginner forex book, just know that like stock trading you have the choice to place options, and even look at ETF products to diversify your portfolio. You are going to learn more about bull and bear markets in a later chapter. For now, know that a bull market is an uptrend and a bear market is a downtrend, and there will be different ways of trading in these markets.

Risk-Reward Ratio

The risk reward ratio is the term used to explain how much a trader is willing to risk in order to gain a reward. Many consider a 1:2 or 1:3 risk reward ratio. It is a statistical calculation. What do you get when you have 80/40? It is 2, right? So in statistics it would mean 2:1, thus you have a reward of 2 versus a risk of 1; meaning if you invest 40 and gain 80, you doubled your investment. In the same way, if you invested 40, but lost half of it, then you risked half your investment. You have to determine the percentage of your investment you are willing to lose.

Profit/Loss

Profit/loss is about calculating whether you have an overall profit for the year or if your losses are overtaking your actual profit. Obviously, profit means you have gains based on what you have invested. If you invested $1,000 and made $100, then you have gained $100. But what if you invested $1,000 again, and you lose $50 on the second trade. Your profit/loss is then $50, where you gained $50 total based on the two trades you placed. At the end of the year, you want to assess whether or not you have actually earned money or lost money. Since you are attempting to gain a profit, you want your overall transactions to show a profit.

Most traders want to see 60/40 in the first year of forex trading, with an increase to 90/10, meaning you have a 60% profit for total trades, and see only a 40% loss during the year. Out of 100%, you still have a profit, and as you get better at trading, you want your profit percentage to increase, while your loss percentage decreases. It would mean your trading plan with an appropriate strategy is becoming more refined.

Trading Plan

A trading plan is an entry, exit, and protection strategy you employ to minimize your losses. This will be explained in greater detail in trading psychology.

Enjoying your eBook so far? Take a moment to subscribe to our FREE newsletter for incredible discounts, books giveaways, and VIP offers!

- ➢ http://www.connectionbooksclub.com/bonus/

All we need is your email, and you'll be set up to receive more of the eBooks you can't wait to read.

Trading Psychology

Trading in the forex market requires an understanding of several pieces because you are trading in pairs, instead of trading for shares of one company. There is a great deal of risk and a high chance of making mistakes if you don't understand the basics of forex trading. A part of those basics is trading psychology.

Trading psychology is defined as your emotional state when trading. Your mindset is going to determine if you are successful or not when you buy and sell currencies. It goes along with knowledge, experience, and skills.

- Confidence
- Danger of Emotions
- Fear
- Greed
- Trading Rules
- Trading Plan

What is Confidence?

What does the word confidence suggest to you? Does it mean you feel comfortable, capable, and intelligent? People who have confidence know they have the knowledge, experience and skills to be successful. People who lack confidence generally do not feel they have skills, experience, or knowledge to accomplish something correctly. This applies in trading.

For you to be confident and capable, you have to have the confidence that you know everything you need to know to be successful, as well as the experience of trying various strategies to ensure you have the skills it takes to place trades appropriately.

In forex, you can develop the skills you need by practicing with a paper money account. You can also build your confidence with such an account. Aside from testing what you are learning, you can also read books that help you develop strategies and learn from experienced traders. By following through with the suggestions you are going to learn in various chapters, you will begin to develop the knowledge, experience, and skills you need to succeed on your trades with an appropriate profit-loss ratio.

The Danger of Emotions

Trading is an unemotional world. Currencies do not have emotions. They are assets that weaken or strengthen based on numerous variables. It is like putting your faith in a robot, thinking that they understand the word "faith." When you bring emotions to the world of trading, you are setting yourself up for failure. Emotions allow you to skew information and data. Let's say, you place your first trade using your money in the forex market. You make $100,000 by investing $100,000. So, in essence, you doubled your money. You would probably be jumping for joy, right? You would feel like you need to get into another trade and repeat this, only you rush in, and the next time, you lose half your investment, which was $200,000.

Your emotions can cause you to make mistakes. Your emotions can also put you on a roller coaster of ups and downs, where you end up with a higher loss instead of a higher profit.

Your trading psychology needs to be developed on the basis that you are going to let your emotions go – good or bad – in an effort to establish a trading strategy that offers you a profit overall for the entire year.

If you can establish a set trading psychology that you do not deviate from, even when greed and fear try to rule you, then you are going to be more successful than those who let their emotions rule.

Fear and its Trap

Fear is definitely an emotion that can cost you hundreds of thousands of dollars or whatever your currency may be. Fear causes us to do things we normally wouldn't do.

Let's take a non-forex example for a minute. Your computer starts sounding sirens, and a warning message pops up stating your computer has been compromised and you need to call the number on the screen that looks legitimate, because it is using the name of a company you use and trust, like an internet provider. Only that number is to a hacker, who is asking for access to your computer to "fix" the problem. In a fearful moment, you can forget that you should never call that number even though you have read about the scam.

Fear can do the same thing in the forex market. You can have a plan set up, with orders in place to protect your investment, but unless you have a proper trading psychology, you can panic, try to exit out of the position, and gain a larger loss for your trouble.

You cannot succumb to fear if you want to succeed in the forex market.

Greed

Greed is another emotion that is going to get you caught in an endless cycle of loss. Greed usually occurs as an emotion when you have just had a winning strategy that netted you more money than you thought possible. Suddenly, you have a positive profit, plenty to trade with, and you want more. You want to keep going even when the signals show you that it is not going to work out. You stay in too long because you have made a stunning profit. At worst, you will open positions that are going to cause you losses in your attempt to gain more profit. Greed can rule you and lead to your downfall. You can become one of the many forex traders who tell the world that it is too complicated, not worth investing in, and all sorts of other negative words.

Instead of getting into this situation, recognize that greed should not rule you. If you feel the sensation that you need to keep trading, walk away. Let the trading plan you set up function as it should, and take the profit you designed your trading system on.

Above all, learn how to trade like a robot, who looks at the information you are given and makes a decision based solely on the evidence of how the market is going to move. There are tools available to help you with this, as well as practice.

Trading Rules

You are going to set up your own trading rules. Yes, there are certain rules everyone follows. They are:

- First, don't trade in an unstable economy.
- Second, determine a risk-reward ratio you can live with.
- Third, don't invest more than you can afford.

The list goes on, but when it comes to your own personal trading rules, you will have a few things to add to the general list of rules.

Your rules are going to be established for the type of trader you are. It all goes back to the second and third rule: what are you willing to lose and what can you afford to lose?

Each person has a different way of calculating this. Some say you should go with a 1 to 2 rule or other complicated rules. There is an easier way of looking at it.

To help you, here is an example:

You own a home, you have $50,000 in the bank for emergencies, and you have $100,000 to trade. This means your liquid assets are $150,000 total. You also have a home asset, but you don't want to lose your home on a bad trade. So, to avoid touching the assets you need in case of emergency, job loss, and to keep a shelter over your head, you are only willing to put $100,000 into your forex trading account.

You are also unwilling to put all your trading "eggs" into one basket. You do not want to lose the entire $100,000 in one trade, so you are not going to buy a standard lot of $100,000.

You also know that you are unwilling to lose the entire amount on one trade, just to use leverage to enhance your position. Therefore, you are not going to invest a percentage of your capital, but then use leverage to make the lot size larger, which would still risk your entire capital due to the leverage amount needed.

As you can see from the example, there are certain things the "example you" is unwilling to do as a way to avoid loss.

Now, when it comes to investing an amount that you are comfortable with, it will need to depend on the lot size and the cost of that lot size. When using USD accounts, the price of a lot is the same as the lot size. This means 1,000 units are $1,000. For the sake of simplicity, we will proceed as if you have a USD account.

We will also say that you intend on investing $10,000 in a mini lot. The price per pip for a mini lot is $1. If you open a position where the quote currency is 1.3136 and it changes to 1.3137, then you have earned 1 pip or $1 dollar. When the market movement is 100 pips, then you earn $100.

So the question becomes, what are you willing to risk of your money to earn a profit? Are you willing to invest $10,000 without leverage? Or knowing that you have $100,000, are you willing to use $2,000 and your broker's leverage option?

If you use the leverage option, know that you are still risking the other $8,000; it is just that if you make a profit off the trade, then you did so without investing the full amount, while if you lose money, you will have to dip into your capital to repay the broker.

This is why you need to establish the trading rules based on how much you are willing to risk versus the potential reward. Only you can determine what you are willing to lose based on market movements. If you have a trading plan that is based on tight losses, you may not be able to make huge profits, but you may be able to limit your losses to a more comfortable level.

With risk-reward, the more you risk, the higher the reward usually is; however, it also means higher losses when things go awry.

As you learn about trading strategies, you will learn how to set your trading rules.

Trading Plan

Trading plans are designed around your trading rules and market movements. Your trading plan will be determined around how much you are willing to risk of your money and any leverage you use. A trading plan is set up based on entry and exit points which you pre-establish before ever entering the trade.

It is also based on the market movements. For example, if you can predict that a currency pair is going to earn 100 pips, then you might establish an entry strategy to enter with a market order. When the position is open, you then put in a second order based on your exit strategy. You have determined not to be greedy, so you put in an order to sell or close the position where you make a profit of 80 pips. Yes, you lose out on 20 pips, but what if the market moves against you, instead of as per your prediction? You would have a loss instead of a profit.

As you set up your trading plan, you will also have something some call a "protection order" or a "stop loss order." The protection order is a secondary order that will automatically close out your position if the market moves against you. What if you could follow the market movement, within a certain pip range? For example, if you open a position at 1.3136, where you expect to earn 100 pips, but you do not want to lose more than 20 pips or $200 on the trade, what could you do? You could set a trailing stop loss. The trailing stop loss would be set at 1.3116. When you start earning pips, say up to 40 pips, so the quote is now 1.3176, the trailing stop is set at 1.3156. It maintains a 20-pip distance, so if the market starts to move against you, you still close the position with a profit. However, if the market does not go in an uptrend, but turns around, then you will sell before the price drops below 1.3116.

Planning your trade ensures that you also set up your trade to automatically sell out, where you don't have to make changes or give in to your fear that you will have a high loss. It is only when you change your trading plan mid-trade that you can suffer from increased losses.

To Sum It Up

Trading psychology is how you will trade for a profit based on controlling your emotions, avoiding fear and greed, and establishing a profitable way to trade based on your trading style. A trading strategy and style that works for someone may be too high-risk or too low-risk for your comfort. This is why you follow the rules that fit your trading requirements, as well as establish a plan based on those rules. There are certain mistakes and general trading rules that all traders follow, and as long as you are within those rules and your own set of rules, then you will lower your losses and increase the potential profits you can make in the forex market. It is all in how confident you are as a means of reducing the negative emotions that can cause you to act quickly and without thought.

What To Do In A Bull Or Bear Market

You already understand that a bull market is an uptrend, when trader confidence is high. You also know that a bear market is a downtrend, where many are not confident in the economy and expect major losses. You understand that you have alternatives, such as trading "options" to try and earn money based on the downtrend in the market. But what do you truly do in a bull or bear market when it comes to forex? Let's take a look.

- Buy in a Bull Market
- Sell in a Bear Market
- Stock Trading vs. Forex

The general stance for traders is to buy when there is a bull market. It is less risky to purchase an asset when the market is positive because you can follow the uptrend to profit and put in protection orders to avoid high-risk situations. It is also assumed by traders that the uptrend will continue and not turn around quickly.

In the same way, you are supposed to sell or close open positions in a bear market because it is unfavorable and there will be more volatility. Many new traders exit the market and wait for favorable conditions they can understand. There are others who are more advanced who decide to sell short or buy options to hedge their bets on what the market will do, and make profit from that.

This principle works in the stock market. In the stock market, you are trading in company shares, which either go up or down as a single entity. If the market is bull, then the stocks should be increasing across the board, including with the indexes that reflect a good market. When the bear market is in place, you know the downtrend is coming, stocks are losing value, and there is a potential to sell short or wait for a new uptrend. Again, it is a single entity you are going to trade.

Stock Trading vs. Forex

Stock trading is different from the forex market. You have a clear up and down trend to see in the entire market. When the Dow Jones and NASDAQ have an up arrow and the NYSE is showing green arrows on stocks across the board, then there is a bull market. If the indexes are showing down arrows, then it means the bear market is in full swing.

Forex doesn't work like that. In fact, there are many professionals who do not believe there is a bull or bear market in forex because it is always both. If the USD is in a downward trend, then the USD is losing value against another currency, which means that you need more USD to buy the other currency, and that's essentially a bull market in the second currency.

If you have an uptrend and a downtrend at the same time in a currency pair—how can you be experiencing a bull or bear market?

The other side of the coin is that in general, a stable global economy will provide value increments across the board for currencies. So it is a bull market, where you determine which currency is gaining value at a faster rate than another. If the economy is unstable, then the value of currencies is decreasing across the board, so you need to determine which currencies are losing value faster than the others. You would then be investing in a bear market, if you believe this line of thought.

A popular saying in trading rooms applies to individual forex traders as well: "Bulls make money. Bears make money. Pigs get slaughtered."

To Sum It Up

For most forex traders, even beginner traders, it is better not to consider forex as a bull or bear market. Rather, assess the stock market as bull or bear. If the stock market is looking favorable, then you know there is investor confidence, which means there will be more volume and liquidity in the financial markets. You can also assess the economy as stable for the currencies that are showing a bull market. You do not want to waste time thinking about bull or bear markets in terms of currency pairs.

You can assess currency pairs in other ways to determine if an up or down trend is going to occur. It does have to do with economic stability, but given that you can invest, whether or not a base currency is going to increase or decrease in value based on the rate it is increasing or decreasing against the quote currency, you want to focus on the actual "rate" versus the bull or bear concept.

Enjoying your eBook so far? Take a moment to subscribe to our FREE newsletter for incredible discounts, books giveaways, and VIP offers!

> http://www.connectionbooksclub.com/bonus/

All we need is your email, and you'll be set up to receive more of the eBooks you can't wait to read.

Fundamental Trading Analysis

Fundamental trading analysis is just one of the four principles of forex trading. A second one is technical analysis, which will be discussed in a different chapter. Fundamentals are based on economic reports, stability, news, and major world events.

- Economic Reports
- News
- Major Events
- Bringing it all together

Some forex investors live on fundamental trading analysis for their strategies. They do not feel there is a basis in technical analysis to provide a true outlook for investing. It is actually a mixture of the two that can provide a good picture, but each will be explained separately.

Economic Reports

Fundamental analysis is in part based on economic reports that each country generates to show a weak or strong economy. There are three reports that are often focused on: inflation rate, economic growth rate or GDP, and employment. The employment report is based on high or low numbers of job creation and layoffs.. Are there a lot of people out of work? Have more jobs been created recently for those who were out of work? If unemployment numbers are down, then it means the economy is getting better. It generally includes both raw numbers of jobs and layoffs and unemployment as a percentage of the working population.

One thing you have to be wary of is when those reports are released. In the holiday months, often starting about October through January, unemployment numbers are down. Places are hiring for the holidays, which helps to reduce these numbers. However, at other times of the year, layoffs from the holidays can increase the unemployment numbers. Of course, it only matters if the volume disagrees with the numbers. If everyone is talking about trading because the unemployment numbers are down, then it means there will be more investors looking to get into the market.

You also need to know what a positive employment rate is all about. Each country has a report that will come out each month. If the USA is releasing the report on the first Friday of each month, and then the EU releases their report on the third Friday of each month, then you might expect the USD to increase in value, thus showing a downtrend for the first two weeks of the month. During the third week, if the EU is expected to have startlingly low unemployment numbers, then the USD may lose value against the EUR – thus an uptrend will occur.

It's important to remember, however, that strong economic reports can have differing impacts depending on both market expectations and where you are in an economic cycle. An employment report that is objectively strong but not as strong as anticipated - either by analysts or by market rumor - can cause a currency to weaken. A strong report can also cause concern about potential interest rate hikes, which can push stocks lower and may drag a currency with it.

As stated though, there are other economic reports that can factor into the macro-fundamental analysis one performs. The inflation rate is considered an overall indication of whether the economy is performing well or losing strength. During the 2007 to 2008 mortgage crisis, the USD lost value even though inflation started to fall. The USA was overinflated, but the financial struggle made it undesirable to trust in the USD. The inflation rate cannot be falling too quickly or rising too quickly, but rather moving at a moderate pace, showing a stable increase or decrease in prices based on the needs of the nation to generate funds, goods, and services.

The growth rate is important because one has to examine if the country's economy is not growing, stable, or growing. More growth usually means there is a demand for currency in order to pay for the growth. It can ensure the currency is valued more. However, it can lead to increased inflation which can weaken a currency, so none of these indicators can be looked at in isolation.

You have learned that economic activity plays a significant role in whether or not a currency increases, decreases, or remains about the same in value. These reports are a part of the equation to show what is happening in the economy. However, you cannot just look at these three reports. You also need to assess things like interest rates.

Are short and long term interest rates increasing or decreasing? Central banks increase short-term rates when the economy strengthens and inflation is increasing or considered likely to increase.

Long-term rates are governed by investment flows into and out of government bonds. These flows can be influenced not just by domestic economic strength or weakness but by international considerations as well. The U.S. dollar and the Swiss franc are currencies that are considered safe havens in times of uncertainty. Money flows into their bond markets when it exits less stable countries; this pushes long-term rates lower and the related cash flows also impact currency rates.

Fundamentals also look at supply and demand. Think back to your economic lessons in school. If you had a high supply of a good, then the value would decrease. If the demand was high, with a low supply, then the value would increase. If supply and demand were balanced, then the value would remain the same. You can say the same in the forex market.

It means if a large corporation is exporting a good to an international corporation, then the international corporation will need to pay for those goods. They will most likely do so in the country of origin's currency. They will trade their domestic currency for the exporting company's currency, thus their domestic currency supply increases, the demand decreases, and the inverse is true for the export company's currency. It means you need to know what the big corporations are doing and whether there is going to be a big movement of funds to satisfy exports and imports.

News

The news shares the economic reports, financial information about governments, and large import/export deals corporations may be making. However, the news may not report everything. You also have news channels like CNBC that look for decent companies to invest in for stocks, with very little to say about currencies. On all these sites, you have to sort through the news and discover what may impact the currencies you are interested.

You have to read between the lines and assess the person who is presenting the news. Is that person skewing information for their investment benefit? Do you want to follow what the herd may be doing or look at other indicators to see if you can make a profit? There is a danger in following everyone else. The masses could be incredibly wrong about what is going to happen. The self-fulfilling prophecy being set by the newscaster may also be unfulfilled and wipe you out if you listen. You are better off looking at the news as just a small piece of the puzzle and to gain global insight on possible movements in the market.

Major Events

Wars are major events. Earthquakes are devastating major events too, which can all affect the currency market. Whenever something unexpected happens to a country, where it is large enough to create fear in the hearts of many, the financial market will react. With terrorist attacks, financial markets may close for the day to prevent a market crash. If the markets close, then your order may not be fulfilled, or you may find a huge loss when the market opens again. Unfortunately, you cannot predict major events. You just have to be aware that you need to check the global market, see if there is anything in the news that has happened or might happen, and determine if you want to invest for the day.

Once again, I remind you that the fact that these types of events cannot be foreseen or predicted contribute to the importance of leaving orders, especially stop-loss orders to protect you when you may not be able to execute a transaction yourself.

Putting it all Together

For fundamental analysis, you are going to look at more than economic reports. You are looking at how the government is structured, if it has enough cash reserves, or a high deficit. You are also going to look at news and major events to determine what could affect the trading day. Once you look at everything and have an understanding of the government behind the currency, you can determine the indicators and whether there are any false indicators of a trend in the currency pair.

You always need to start out with a macro-examination of the currency pairs, then reduce it to a micro-examination based on the current day. If you do not start out with a global outlook, you could be missing some important data that will impact how you are able to invest your funds. You could see significant losses.

Enjoying your eBook so far? Take a moment to subscribe to our FREE newsletter for incredible discounts, books giveaways, and VIP offers!

> ➢ http://www.connectionbooksclub.com/bonus/

All we need is your email, and you'll be set up to receive more of the eBooks you can't wait to read.

Technical Trading Analysis

Technical trading is one of the four basic principles of forex. It is one way you can assess the market and determine how you wish to trade. There are two schools of thought, and you already learned about fundamental analysis. You know that it is far better to use both fundamentals and technical data to determine how the market might move. There are also many traders who believe that you should only trade on technical data and forget about fundamentals. You can decide for yourself, but keep in mind what could happen if you are missing a piece of the forex puzzle.

- Assessing the Charts
- Moving Average
- Support and Resistance
- Breakout Trend

Technical charts show past data. You can look at what happened five years ago, a year ago, six months ago, three months ago, a month ago, a week ago, or even yesterday. You can examine what happened an hour ago. But what you cannot know for certain is what is going to occur in the next hour, in the next week, or in the next month. An earthquake in Italy can upset the entire European market, cast a shadow on the value of the euro, and cause it to lose value against the USD, where it might otherwise have continued to gain against the dollar.

For this reason, you may not want to solely predict how the market is going to move based on technical data alone. Yes, self-fulfilling prophecies have been known to happen. You gain data that shows there is enough volume and interest in a currency pair to make a trend breakout or continue. It is a falsehood that can have you thinking your prophecy will work this way each time. Rather than get caught in such a cycle, it is best to look at the big picture and then narrow the picture as you assess all aspects of the market.

There are three simple concepts to assess for technical trading: moving averages, support and resistance, and breakout trends. You can look at these three technical analysis options using standard charts or candlestick charts. For beginners, it is often better to assess the standard price charts that show the momentum of a currency pair versus trying to learn what candlestick charting is all about.

Before discussing the typical trend assessments forex traders use, let's understand the price chart.

Price Charts

A price chart is a plotted graph of quote currency rates. Depending on the time frame, you may see extremely detailed exchange rates or fewer details. For example, if you look at a 5-year chart, then the trends are going to be based on each year, where you may see an uptrend for the entire year, but when you zoom into that specific year, you see up and downtrends.

When you look at a single day, you can see hourly trends that do not appear on the weekly chart as clearly. Forex trading is about choosing a time frame to trade in, based on the potential trend. If you want to trade on an uptrend, then you need to know if the time frame of 10 minutes or an hour shows the uptrend indicators, or if the prediction is for a reversal of the trend.

Let's use an example: EUR/USD on a Monday. We have decided to look at 4 hours, from the opening of the New York market till noon. When the market opened, the EUR/USD was in an uptrend, where the USD was increasing at an exchange rate from 1.3136 to 1.4136. Now, you are going to trade in the afternoon. There are three indicators on the chart showing a reversal of the trend is about to happen. You do not want to click the offer because it would mean buying the EUR and selling the USD. Instead, you want to ride the downturn so you select the bid price to sell the EUR and buy the USD. However, it turns out that the overall weekly trend was an uptrend. Rather than the indicators being correct, the exchange rate continued to increase in numerical value going from 1.4136 to 1.5136. You lost 0.1 pips because you bet against the current trend.

The time frame is important to assess what is actually happening. If you look at a narrow time frame, you might miss something.

Moving Average

A moving average is designed to help you see a period of time in a smoother way. There are often fluctuations in the exchange rate for a currency pair, and these fluctuations can hide the overall trend. By assessing a specific period of time, you can look for changes in the trend, as well as indicators that show a clear uptrend or downtrend.

The disadvantage with moving averages is the potential for false signal reads. You have smoothed out market movements, so you may not see an indicator that is telling you that the trend is not going to go as you think it will. For moving averages, you need to know that the number of reporting periods that you include in your moving average calculation will affect the moving average line on the price chart. Also, the fewer data points used in the calculation, the closer the moving average will stay to the spot rate for that period, which reduces the value of information and insight into the market movements. If you have a moving average that follows the spot rate too closely, you are not going to be able to recognize reversal points and may incur more losses.

The simple moving average is the one to pay attention to as a beginner, since it is the easiest to understand. This moving average is calculated from a series of price points, where you add the prices together, then divide the total by the number of data points you used. The SMA, as it is known by professionals, will show you a certain period of time such as 15 rates, which means when a new exchange rate is published, the calculation drops the first rate and adds the new one to keep the SMA going. Most traders use 20 price points in their calculation to create a strategy that works best.

For advanced strategists, the weighted moving average is used more often. The WMA is a calculation done in the same manner as the SMA; however, it is linearly weighted, where you have the most recent rates offering a greater impact on the trend. The oldest rate in the calculation is weighted 1, whereas the newest is weighted 3. Some traders find this offers a more relevant trend, where they can see better fluctuations in price to indicate a reversal or continuation of the trend.

SMA traders find that the noise reduction with too many fluctuating rates helps them see trends and reversal points, but you may also be slower to react.

Support and Resistance

Support and resistance is a type of trend you can see on the price charts. For most individuals, it is the most accurate to trade with because you can predict the lows and highs of the currency pair within a certain point of reference. The support is the low line, it is what a downtrend will bounce off of and reverse into an uptrend. The resistance line is the high, which is where the uptrend will bounce and turn back into a downtrend. Some currency pairs will bounce throughout the day between the support and resistance because investors are getting in and out to earn money from the pip changes as the price increases and decreases.

When the support level is reached, you buy into the currency pair. You ride the uptrend and then close out of your position by selling. Some investors are savvy enough to sell out of their position, but sell more than they originally bought. They create a short sale, so they ride the trend back to the support and buy in. The difference from the resistance to the support, is still a change in pips that can provide earnings since you sold one to gain the quote currency.

The reason many beginners trade on the support and resistance is because they know about when the currency will change or reverse from the current trend to a new trend. It is not always the same value, but it will be close enough to allow you to design an entry and exit strategy for maximum benefit. It all comes into play based on the profit and risk you are ready to assume. You will want to have protection orders in place for your strategy to work in the event that something turns against your position in the market.

The fact that many traders follow support and resistance levels can lead to two different and offsetting types of behavior.

First, the fact that "everyone" is looking at a particular support level can become a self-fulfilling prophecy - because people expect the currency to bounce from that level, they buy as it approaches that level, causing the bounce to happen. Second, if the currency breaks through the support, those who expected it to bounce may sell their position and cause the downward move to accelerate.

Breakout Trend

In technical analysis, you can also look for the breakout trends. These are the trends that will leave behind a stagnant position or a support and resistance trend, allowing you to make more money off your trade. You will want to understand the support and resistance trend first before you try to learn the breakout trend.

With the breakout trend, there are indicators, usually three of them that come from news, economic reports, and patterns shown in the price charts. These patterns can be different based on whether the breakout will occur with a reversal trend or be a continuation of a trend.

To Sum It Up

Moving averages, support and resistance, and breakout trends are the top three technical trends you want to study and learn before you move on to more difficult concepts. Once you get these trends down, you can start to look at candlestick charts for things like hammers, and regular price charts for head and shoulders patterns.

Developing A Forex Strategy That Works For You

Plenty of forex strategies are touted as the secret to trading forex in a few minutes to several hours. However, it is important to note that no one strategy is always correct. You may use one strategy for a certain currency pair situation and other strategies for other situations.

- Strategies to achieve better gains
- Strategies to avoid major losses
- Secret strategies of forex trading

Keep in mind your risk aversion, the profit to loss you are willing to accept, and your current knowledge. Test out these strategies to see how successful they are or how you can modify them to fit your trading rules.

Strategies to achieve better Gains

- Start with a limit order, so you are buying at a set price, not the market price that will continue to fluctuate until the order is filled or canceled.
- Predetermine the possible pip gain.
- Set your stop loss, taking profit, or trailing stop loss order.
- Exit the market when you have gained your profit or hit your loss level, do not remain to attempt to make a larger profit or smaller loss.

There are two trends to use for achieving better gains: support and resistance, and breakout trends.

1. Start by analyzing the global economic situation.
2. Narrow the economic information to the currency pair you are interested in trading.
3. Determine if there are any economic reports, major events, or news that could affect a price chart trend you see. A presidential election or discussion about the election can sway a trend in one direction or another.
4. Look for the support and resistance or breakout trend indicators. Do you see three indicators that state to sell or buy a specific currency?
5. Set your order and loss prevention orders.

These two trends work in gaining more profits over time because you always have a pip increase or decrease you are looking for. You set out to make a profit, such as 50 pips per trade, instead of trying to follow the trend all the way until it ends. It offers more consistency versus someone who stays in, taking as much profit as possible on a breakout trend.

Strategies to avoid major losses

There are three orders that keep being mentioned: stop loss, trailing stop loss, and take profit. Each of these orders is designed to help you avoid major losses. The great news—you get to use these strategies, while you are aiming to make a consistent profit, with the support and resistance, and breakout trends.

The **stop loss** order is where you set a specific worst-case level at which to exit your position. You might decide you are willing to lose 10 percent of your invested capital. If you invest $10,000 you would lose $1000 if you have a stop loss order set at 10 percent off the quote currency price. If the market turns around on your position, your order is filled when it reaches the price you have ordered your position to close at. The downside is that you can put the stop loss too tight to the currency rate. You can also lose any profit you gain if the market follows the trend you are trading with and then reverses before you close out of the position.

The **trailing stop loss** is better simply because it follows the current price. If you gain a profit, then the trailing stop loss always keeps a number of pips you decided off the current price. If the market turns against you, your position closes. If it keeps going, you get to make more profit until you set a closing order. It is a matter of comfort.

A **take profit** order helps you with gaining more profit, but also minimizing your losses. You can set an order to remove the profit you have gained, but remain in the position. If you also have a trailing stop loss on your position, then the position closes if the market moves against you. In this way, you have three ways that you can employ the above strategies to gain more profit, as well as minimize what you might lose if the market moves against your position.

Secret strategies of forex trading

Here is one advanced forex trading strategy, you might wish to employ. It is not a secret, except in how you are going to form your strategy around your trading plan. Remember, you decide the risk you are willing to take with your capital.

1. Research the market.
2. Find a currency pair worth investing in.
3. Study the yearly chart, six-month chart, three-month chart, one-month chart, and then the weekly chart.
4. After you have studied the charts for common patterns and indicators, look at the news for the day.
5. Go to the daily chart and see if the indicators are to buy or sell.
6. Check the four-hour chart and see if the indicators are the same for the day or if they are opposite.
7. Next, reduce the chart to an hour. Look for the support and resistance. If it is there, then study the chart to see what occurs in 10-minute intervals.
8. When you have a clear interval to buy because the support level has been hit, buy in.
9. Set your protection orders and exit position.
10. Reap the benefits.
11. Wait for the next ten-minute segment and indicators for the "buy" and buy in again.

Every 10-minute segment can provide you with a profit. It might not be the huge profit that you want, but it is a steady profit over an hour or more. You could do this all day, as long as the volume, volatility and liquidity are in the currency pair to keep the bouncing movement of the price going up to the resistance level and back down to the support level. It may not happen in 10 minutes; it could be in as little as five minutes or over an hour. But, you can consistently make a profit.

Pitfalls To Avoid In Forex Trading

The following are the top pitfalls you want to avoid when you trade forex. They are common issues that many new traders have. It can lead to large capital losses that will ensure you are unable to trade again or will want to trade again. Avoiding the following will at least help you towards setting up strategies with proper entry and exit positions, towards the possibility of gaining more profit than loss overall.

- Increasing Losses: many traders will increase their losses, instead of backing out of a trade. For example, if you can tell the currency market is moving against your position, you should sell out and cut your losses. However, many emotional and beginner traders tend to stay in. They think they can recover if they keep the trade open. Do not fall for this. You will only increase your losses.

- Failure to protect your order: this is another way for you to increase your losses. Rather than protecting your position with a take profit order, trailing stop loss, or stop loss, you simply think you can sell out of any position because you are watching your trade. Unfortunately, just because you place a trade doesn't mean it will fill. You could miss the mark by trying to get an order filled. It is far better to have one in place that automatically fills. These orders are not a complete saving grace for orders, but they are better than trying to get in within a second before you lose 100 pips due to a sudden and swift market turn.

- Not setting up a trading plan: your trading plan is in place to ensure that you have a guide to follow. Even if a part of it doesn't work, you still need to follow the trading plan, so that you are protected from further losses. If you have no plan, then you might be tempted to stay in the trade too long and lose instead of gain.

- Trying to average up or down to recover losses: this is where you are now trying to play catch up. In this situation, you didn't keep to the losing trade, but you are trying to gain more from another trade. You keep placing trades that you expect to cover the losses. You don't want to do this. Instead, go with your strategies. Determine the best position to open and then let your trading plan work for you. You will eventually even out or gain more because you are letting the market work for you, instead of trying to force it.

- Trading too frequently: there are some times the currency market is not worth investing in. Remember the rule about investing when there are two markets open? It is because there is volume and thus momentum in the market. You have to wait for one country to wake up, see the market, and then start investing. You will know when it is time because the volume and liquidity will pick up. These are the hours to trade, versus trying to force a profit off of low volume and little action in the currency pair. Trading means you spend pips as the fee for making the buy or sell order, so you are losing money, if you are only making 1 pip from a transaction.

- Using leverage: you should understand about leverage now, given the explanations in other chapters. Leverage can be great as long as you have the liquidity to cover it, but as soon as you leverage more than you can afford, you are panicking and making one losing trade after another.

- Following others: in some circumstances, following others helps you gain a profitable trade. But, you still have to have your own strategy. Are the concepts someone is discussing going to work for you? Are you actually seeing the same indicators as the herd or not? You need to do your own research, establish a trading plan, and stick to your rules. Just because someone else placed a trade for 100 pips doesn't mean you want to follow. In fact, you might only want to earn 50 pips in profit to ensure you get a profit instead of a loss.

- Not conducting research: using someone else's research or not doing research at all is just as dangerous. You need to conduct research, learn the currency pairs of interest, and invest when there is a reason to do so. Investing when you do not know anything about a currency pair usually turns out in a great loss of capital and turns you against forex completely. Don't let that happen.

- Trading multiple markets: if you are going to trade in forex, then choose a market. Yes, you could trade when Japan opens, sleep, then trade when the UK and USA are open. However, you are better off choosing a specific time to trade, learning how that market time frame works, and trading currencies. If you trade in multiple markets, you are bound to make mistakes. You will be too busy trying to keep the markets straight, researching, and you may not even place a trade because you miss out on the potential entry point. Stick with one market. If you want to eventually trade in more than one market, then at least diversify your portfolio with stocks that you can buy in, sit on long-term, and only monitor once a day to ensure your position is still solid.

- Overconfidence: when a gambler makes a huge win at the tables, they build confidence, so much confidence that they keep playing till they lose all their winnings plus what they came to the table with. You don't want to be this person in the forex market. Confidence is great because you make an entry position; however, if you get overconfident you are bound to make more mistakes or try to repair losses by overtrading when you should step out of the market altogether.

Enjoying your eBook so far? Take a moment to subscribe to our FREE newsletter for incredible discounts, books giveaways, and VIP offers!

> http://www.connectionbooksclub.com/bonus/

All we need is your email, and you'll be set up to receive more of the eBooks you can't wait to read.

Tools That Help Forex Traders

Forex trading tools are there to help you. They are not there to do the investing for you.

- Paper Money Accounts
- Charting Software
- Automated Signals

Paper Money Accounts

Paper money accounts are provided by most brokers. They are accounts that allow you to learn how to trade in the forex market when you are starting out. You can reset your account at any time if you have a loss or completely make a mess of the trades you are making. For some, they think it builds too much confidence, so you become too cavalier when you trade with real money. If you do things correctly, then you will know to leave your emotions out of it and actually manage to learn something.

The point of paper money is to test various strategies. You want to see if something works versus hopping into the market and making a huge mistake.

Charting Software

Charting software allows you to plot indicator lines like support and resistance, SMA, and other trend lines. It is a way for you to learn and to determine if you are truly seeing patterns. For many investors, it is the way to go rather than using brokers who chart for you and provide signals. You can find your own signals and thus have no one to blame if something goes wrong. Of course, you can be wrong, so it is something you need to decide if it will make you more or less comfortable.

Automated Signals

Automated signals are also provided with charting software. If you have charts already generated with SMA or other trends lines, then you can also ask the software to provide you with buy and sell signals. It is a matter of comfort level, again. You may be more comfortable with someone else who has more experience analyzing the market, so you can decide to buy or sell to open a position. If you do not want a lot of risk and trust the software, then you may be more comfortable using it. For some, there is a need for more control in deciding what the signals are. You can find your own signals with non-automated charting software.

Dear Reader,

Connection Books Club wants to thank you for the purchase of one of our many informative eBooks! We hope you enjoyed your purchase and we want to invite you to join our club.

When you subscribe to our FREE club, you'll receive regular newsletters and incredible discounts on our bestselling books! Connection Books Club makes reading easy, giving you the content you want, at a price you can't believe. All that it takes to enroll in our FREE book club is your email. We'll send you the latest business and personal development news and highlight the newest books that are ready for you to enjoy.

➢ http://www.connectionbooksclub.com/bonus/

As part of your subscription, we're giving you a FREE download of one of our favorite eBooks, *Money Management: Learn How to Organize Your Financial Life and Invest in Your Future*. This eBook covers many financial situations, such as lowering interest rates and exploring options surrounding bankruptcy, helping you determine the best financial action for you.

Money management may be difficult for some people, but with your FREE copy of *Money Management: Learn How to Organize Your Financial Life and Invest in Your Future*, you'll learn the skills and information you need to make the best decisions to secure your financial future. The strategies contained in this eBook, designed for the everyday person, offering easy to follow steps and money saving tips.

Understanding money and how to make it works for you is important and with this eBook, you'll learn what you need to know to start building your financial security. Here are the top 5 reasons for reading *Money Management: Learn How to Organize Your Financial Life and Invest in Your Future*:

1. The strategies in this book are designed to help real people achieve their financial goals.
2. Explore different options for retirement.
3. Discover hacks for navigating the grocery store's subtle spending traps.
4. Inform yourself about how you might be able to get away with paying less than you owe on credit cards and other outstanding debts.
5. Experience a feeling of newfound freedom when you understand that you have every ability to live a life of financial stability.

➢ Get your copy here:
http://www.connectionbooksclub.com/bonus/

The benefits of receiving this eBook for FREE are endless! Take control of your finances and start living the life you want.

By subscribing to Connection Books Club, not only will you get incredible discounts, our FREE welcome gift eBook, and a regular newsletter, but you'll also get the opportunity to receive FREE eBooks! Subscribers are invited to share reviews of the eBooks they've read, earning new titles at no cost! All it takes to enroll is your email. http://www.connectionbooksclub.com/bonus/

Discounts and free eBooks are just a click away! Enter your email for VIP access to new books, incredible deals and money saving options, and even free giveaways! And don't forget, by signing up today for Connection Books Club, you'll receive the incredible eBook *Money Management: Learn How to Organize Your Financial Life and Invest in Your Future* for FREE!

Connection Books Club is excited to have you join our ranks of subscribers. We hope you enjoy your FREE eBook and all the great reading coming your way soon!

http://www.connectionbooksclub.com/bonus/

Wrap Up: Forex Overview

Forex for beginners is a monumental amount of information for you to learn. It is reasonable that you probably didn't catch everything right away. Go back and read through things, enjoy the book, and determine what else you need to learn. Stick with resources that are from government sites to help you find brokers, more detailed forex information, and possible strategies.

After you have practiced your strategies with paper money, you can go on to trade with real money.

You will be ready to trade forex, whether you set a position for 10 minutes or several hours.

Thank you for reading this book, and please use it as a guide to help you gain more knowledge for investing in the forex, rather than a gospel to follow for forex strategies.

If you have enjoyed this book, I'd greatly appreciate if you could leave an honest review on Amazon.

Reviews are very important to us authors, and it only takes a minute to post.

Thank you

www.ingramcontent.com/pod-product-compliance
Lightning Source LLC
Chambersburg PA
CBHW060410190526
45169CB00002B/835